MIRROR DRAWING BOTTLES

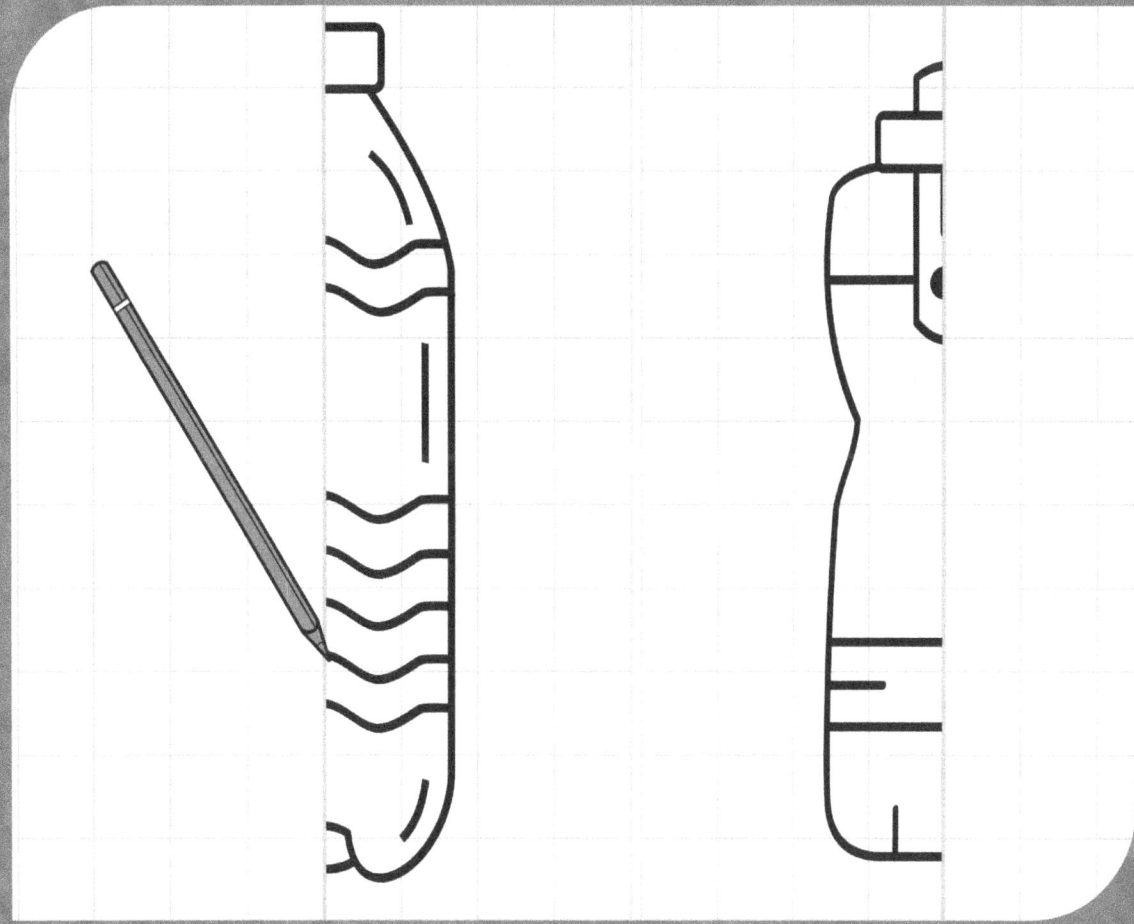

for Kids Aged 3-8

@ Copyright 2021 - All rights reserved.

It is not legal to reproduce, duplicate, or transmit any part of this document in either electronic means or in printed format. Recording of this publication is strictly prohibited and any storage of this document is not allowed unless with written permission from the publisher except for the use of brief quotations in a book review.

This Book Belongs to:

Name: .... Date: ....

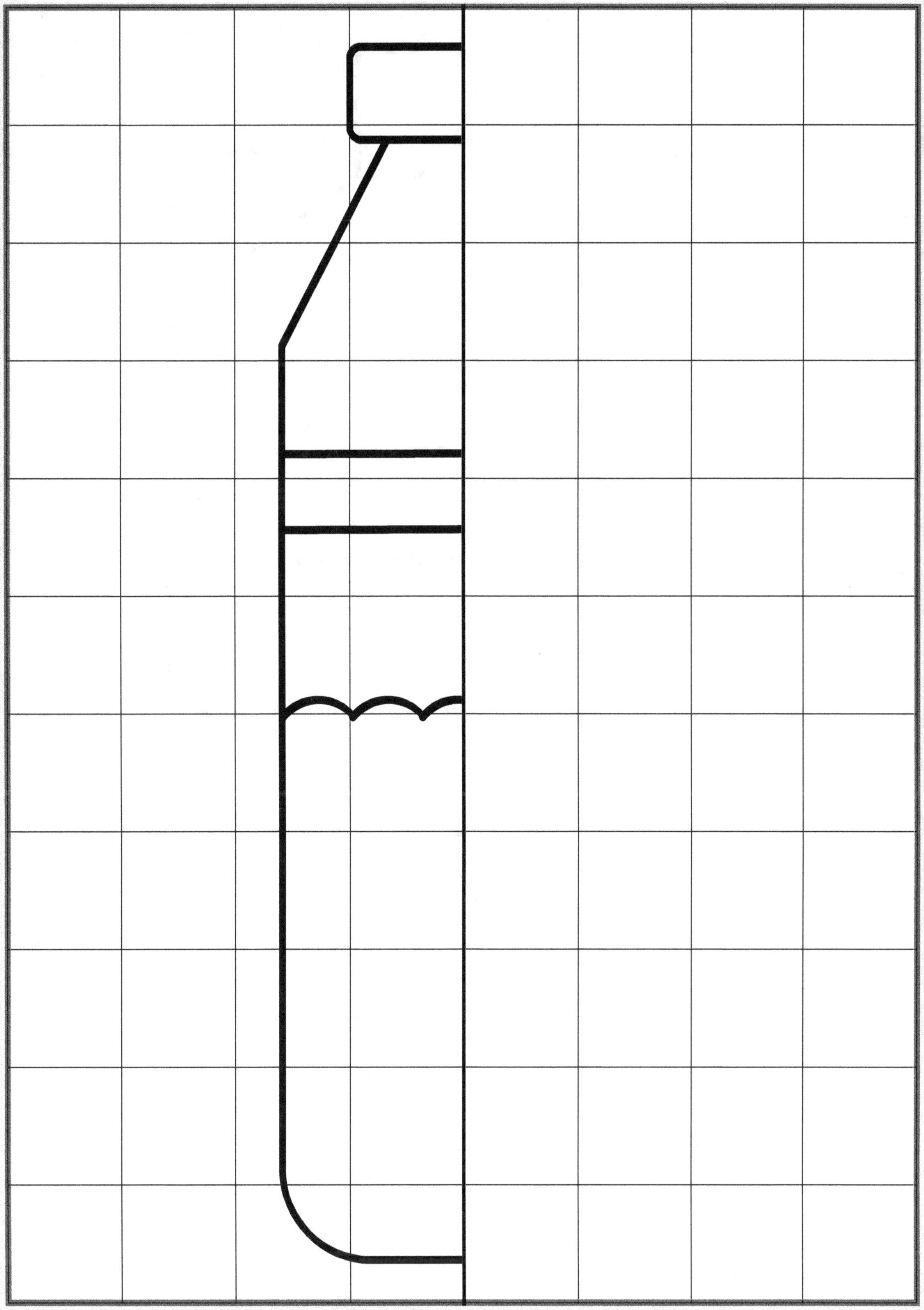

Name: .... Date: ....

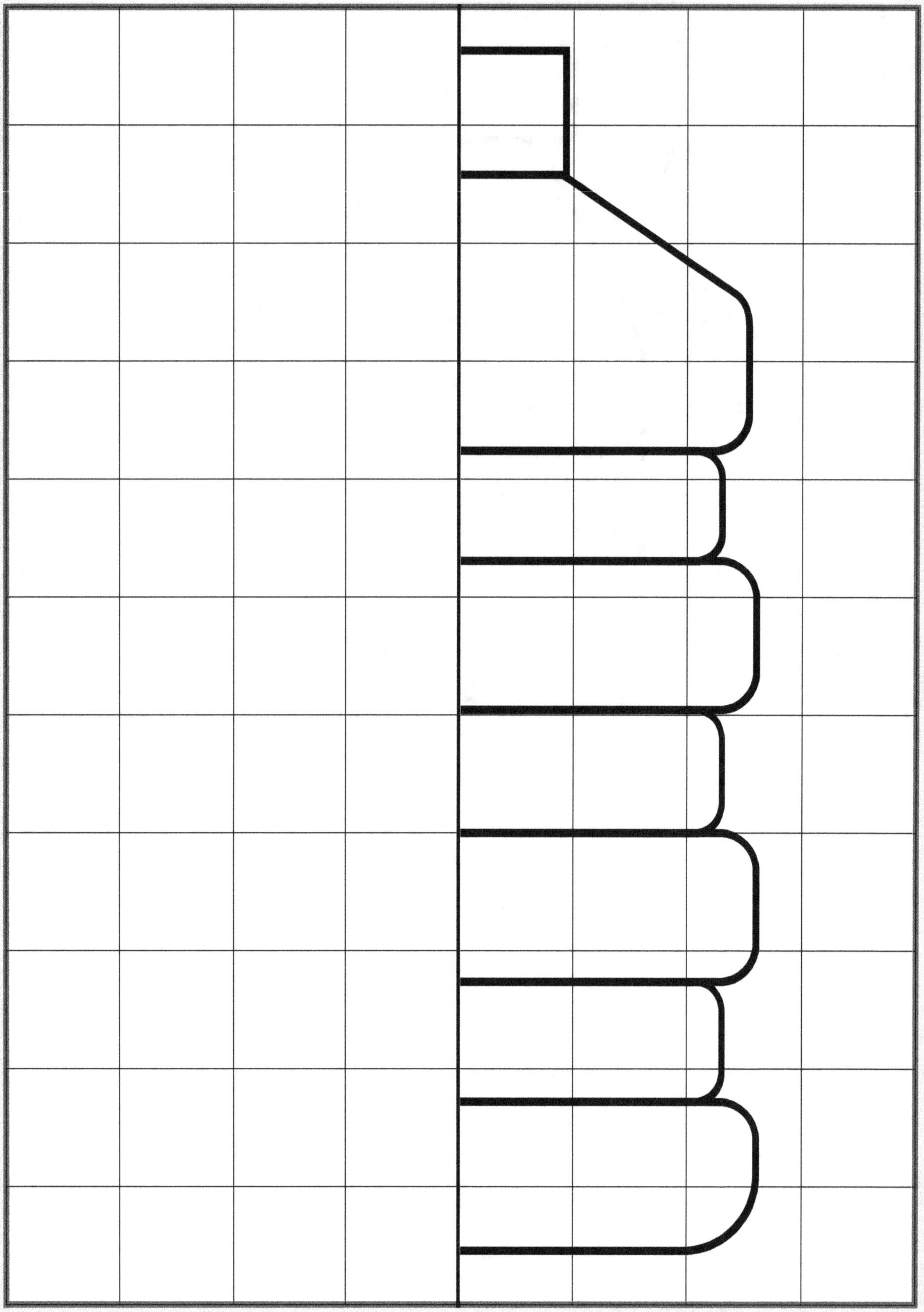

Name: .... Date: ....

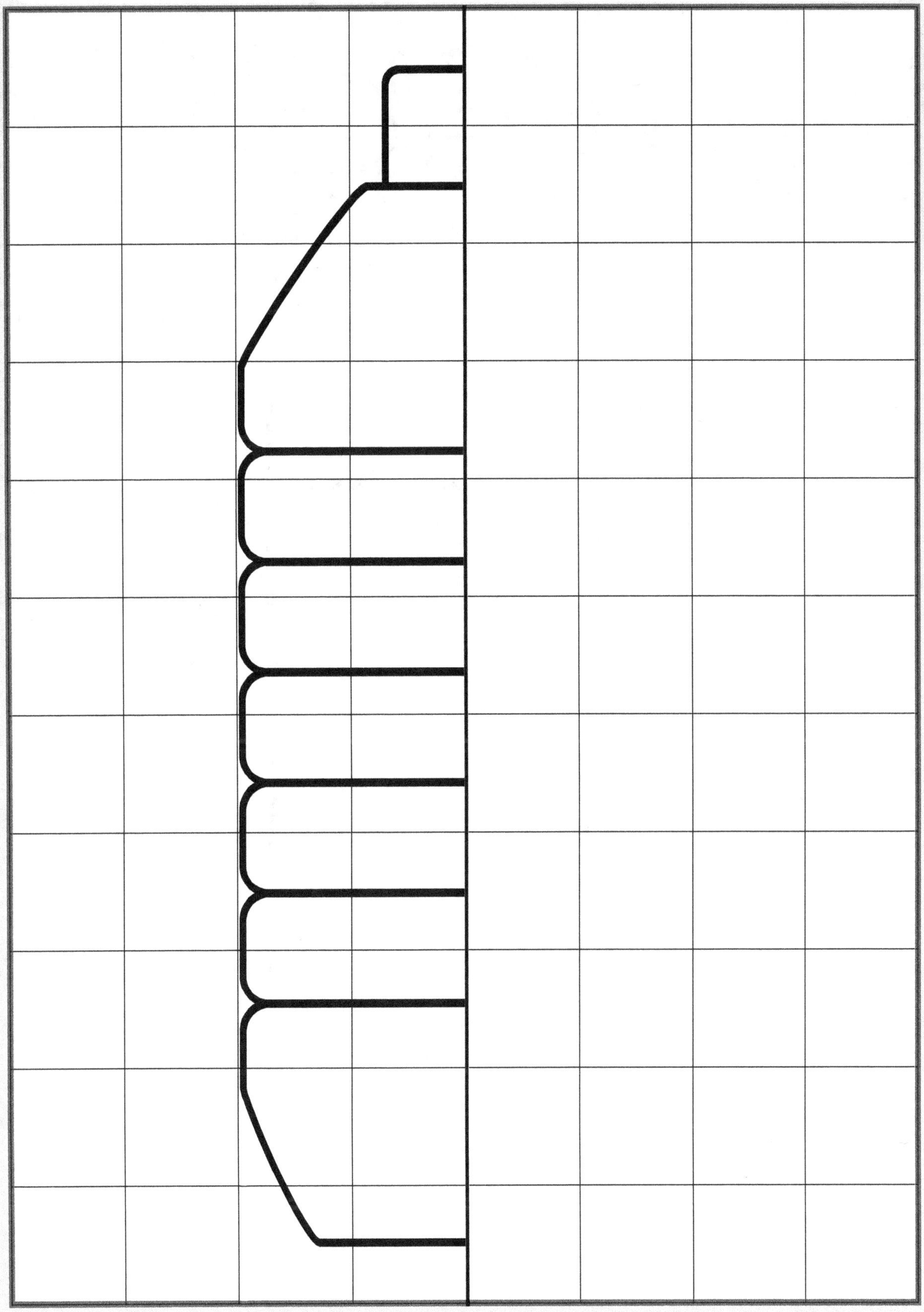

Name: .... Date: ....

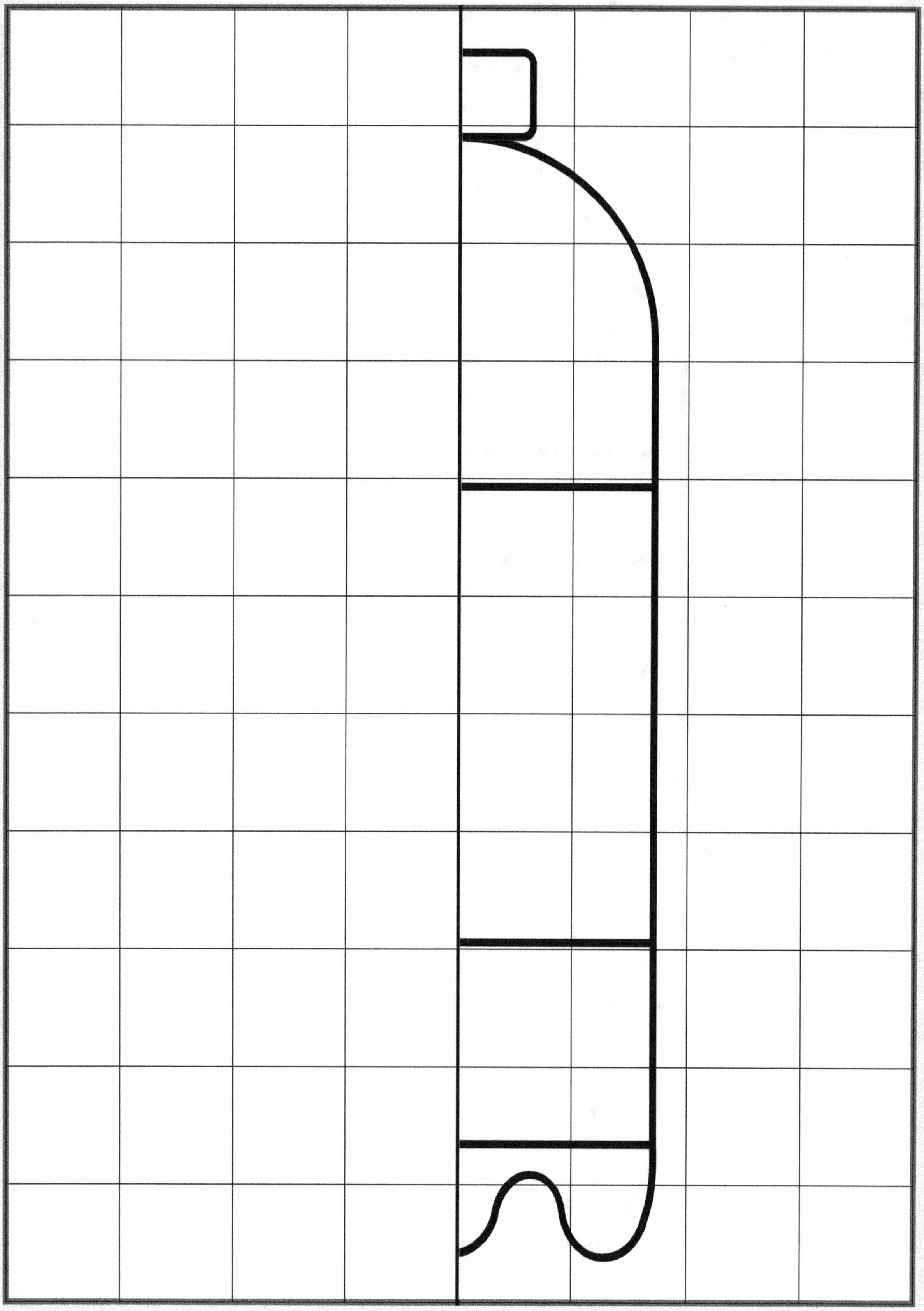

Name: .... Date: ....

Name: .... Date: ....

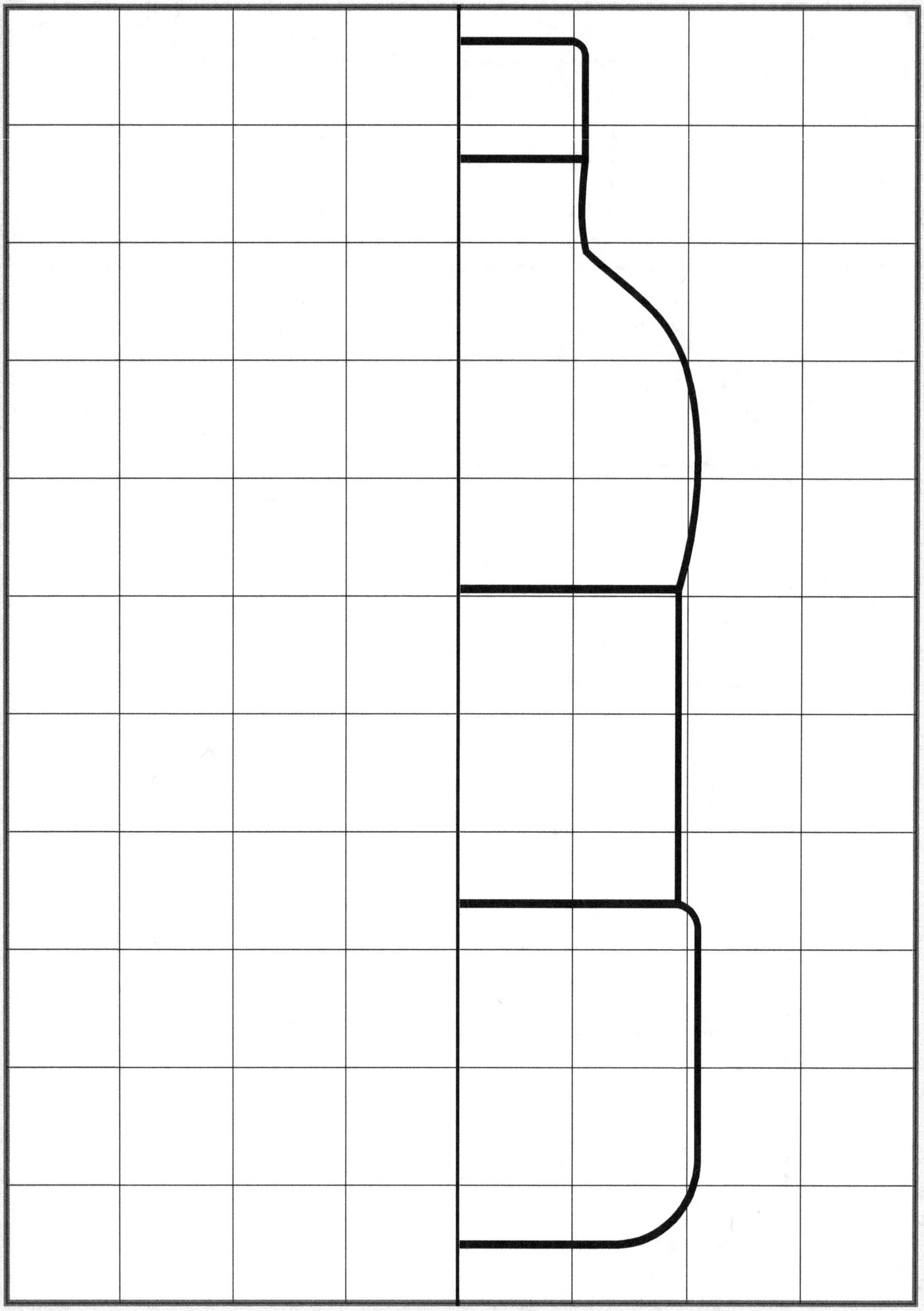

Name: .... Date: ....

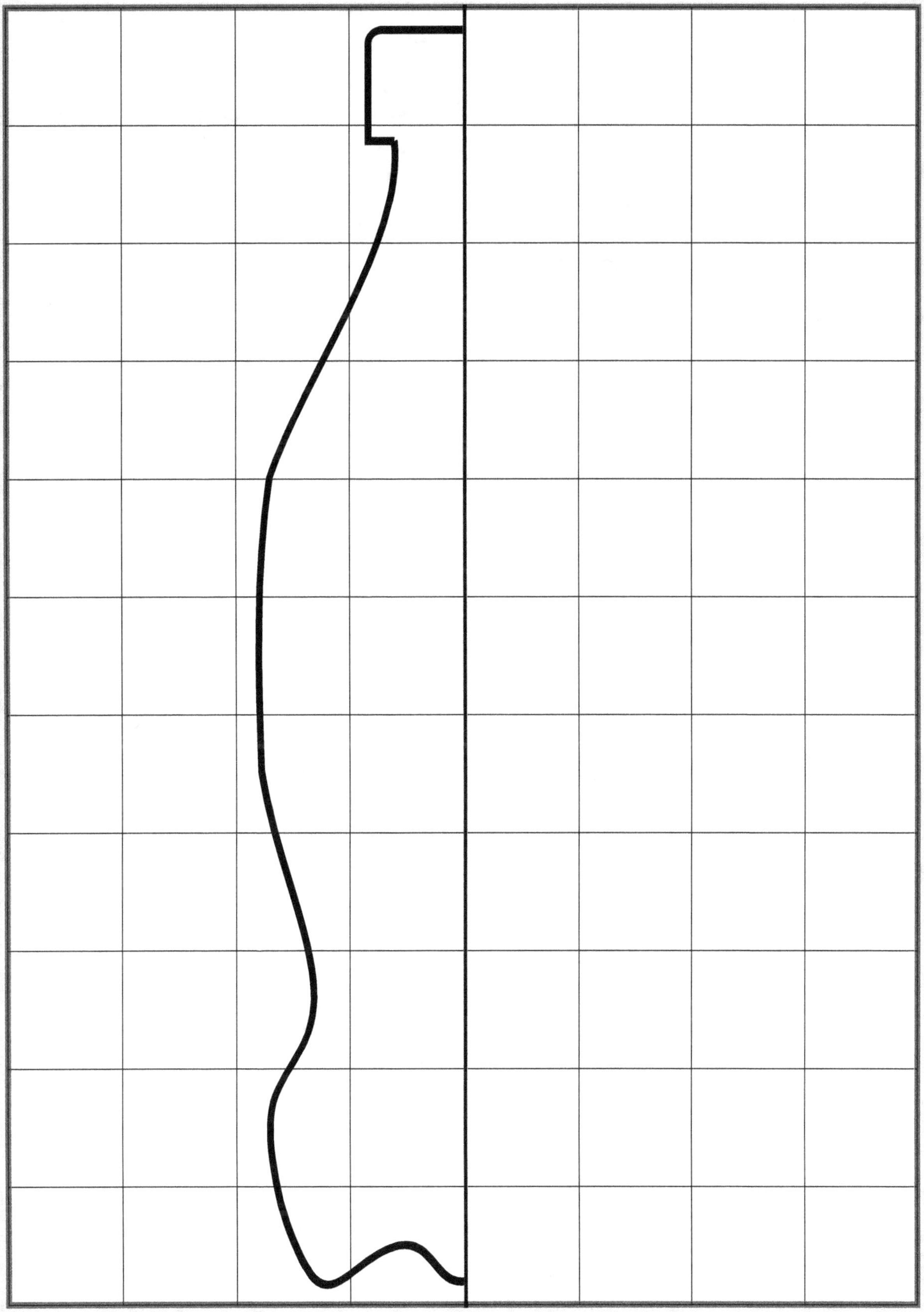

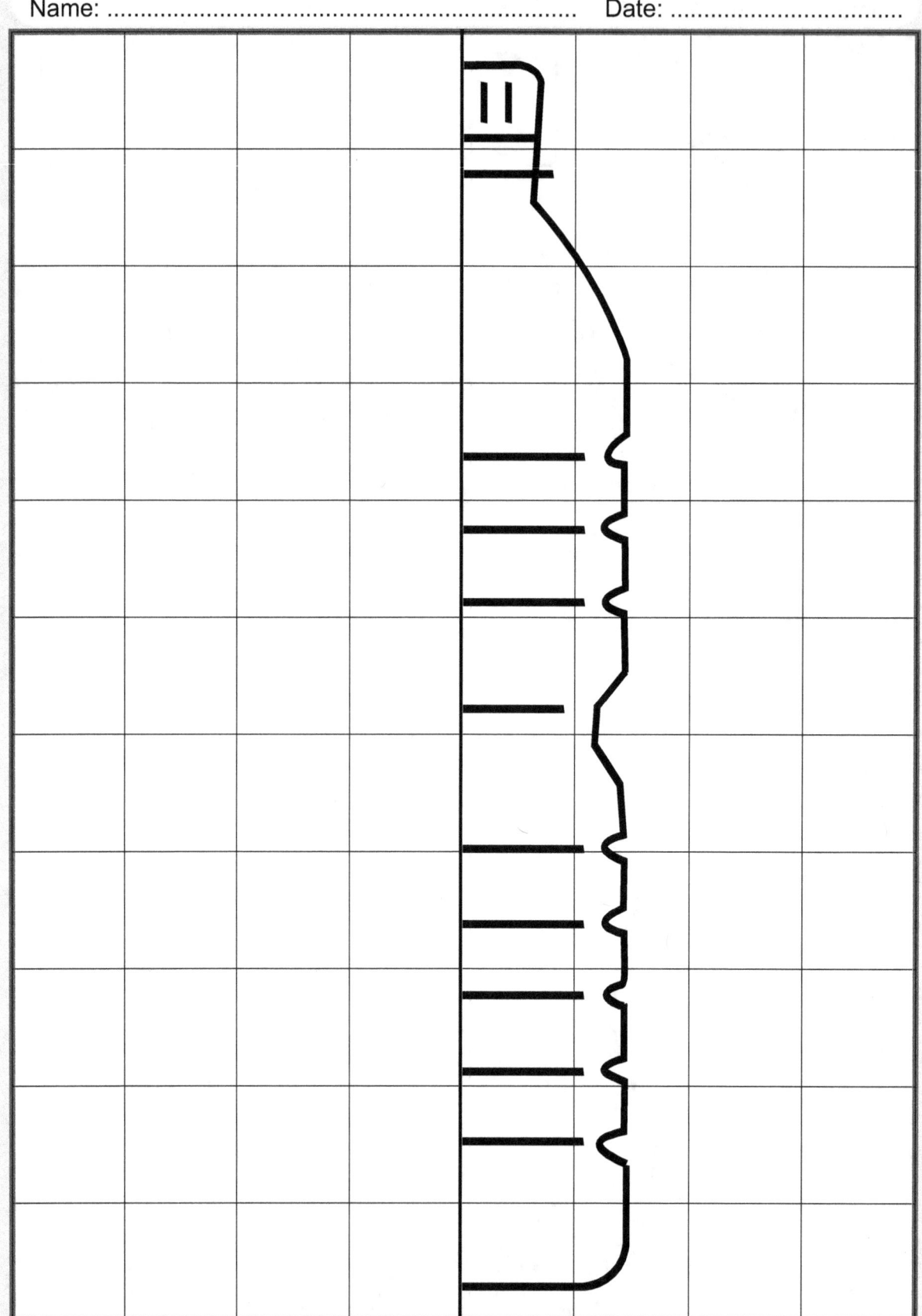

Name: .... Date: ....

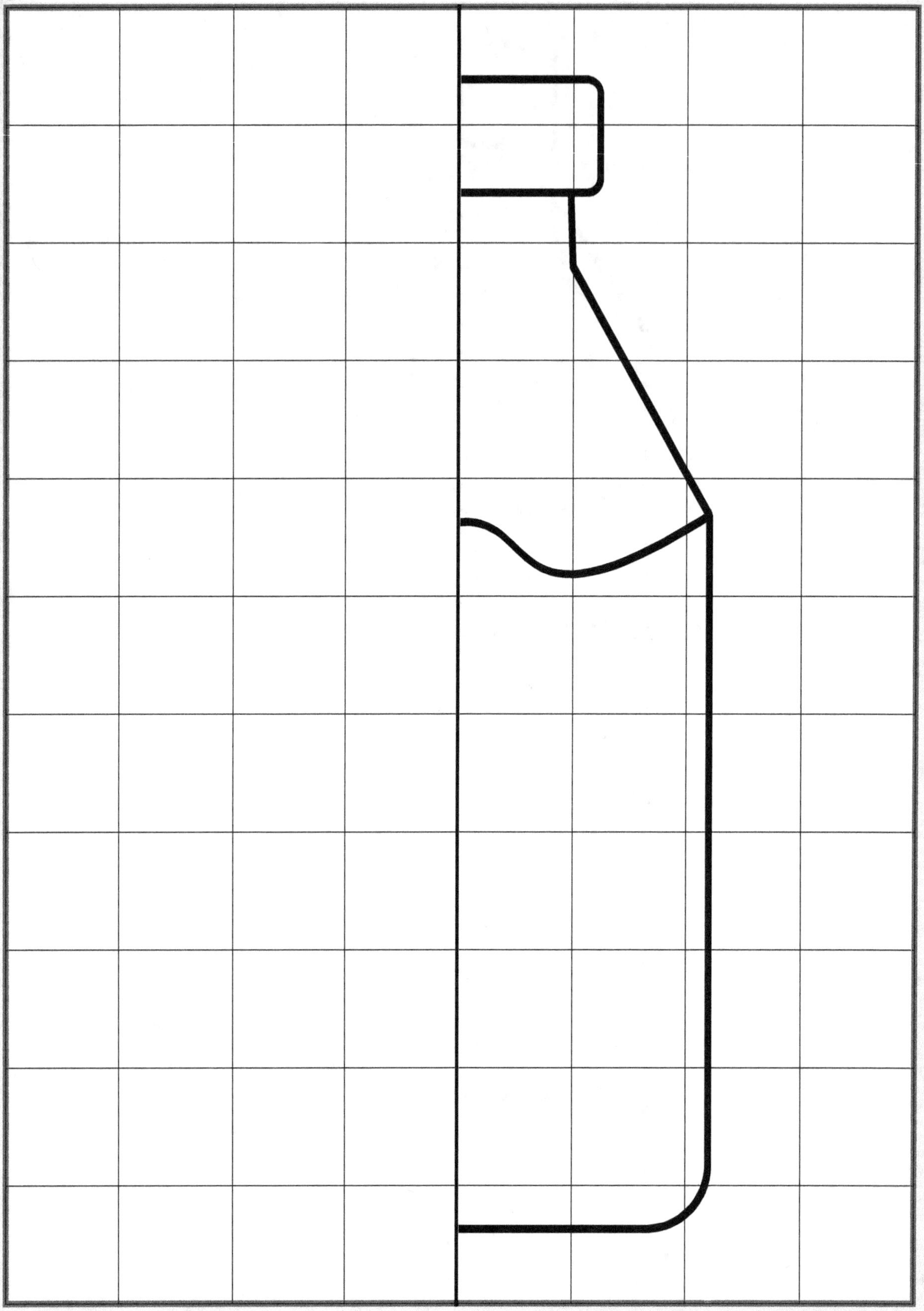

Name: .... Date: ....

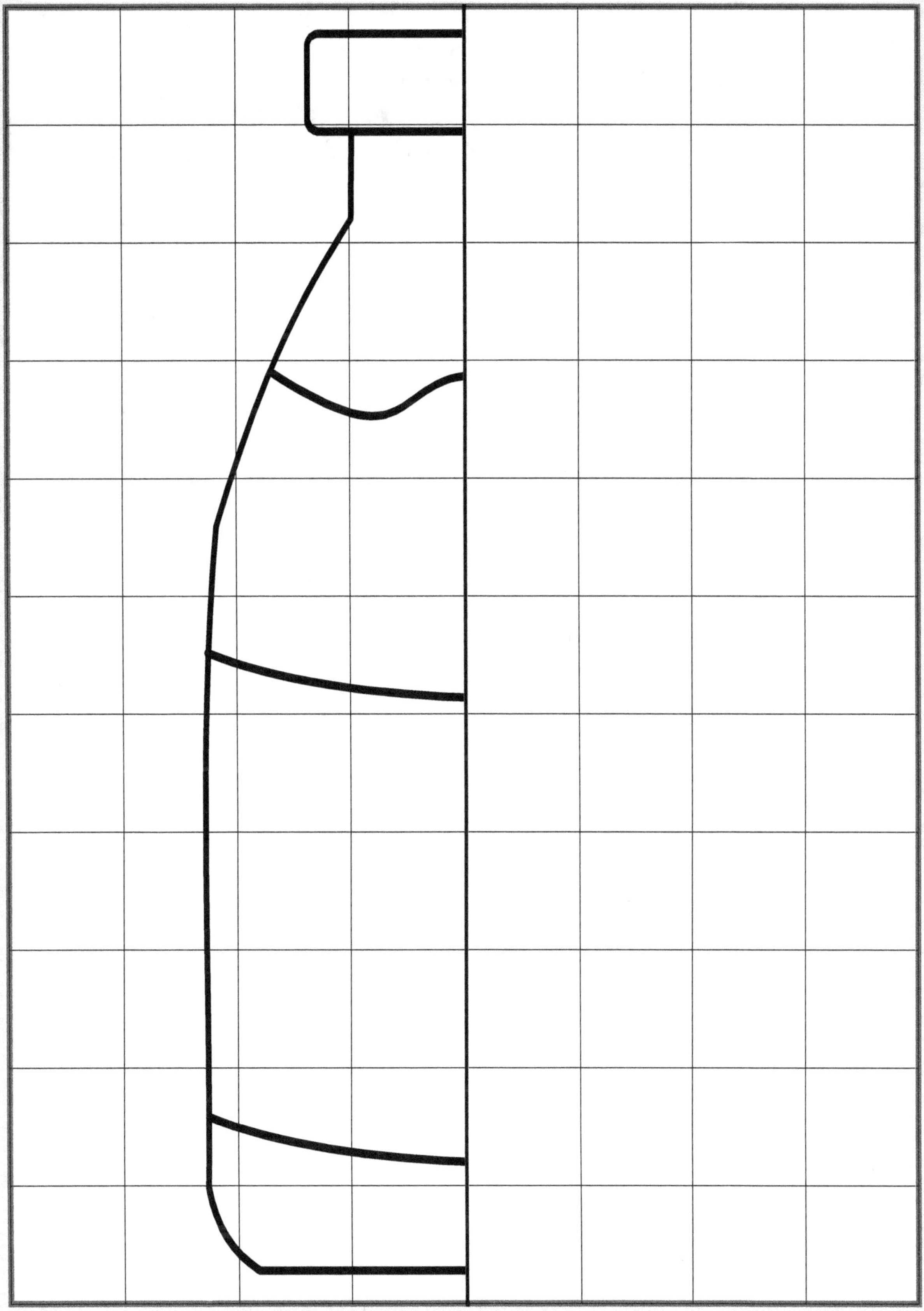

Name: .... Date: ....

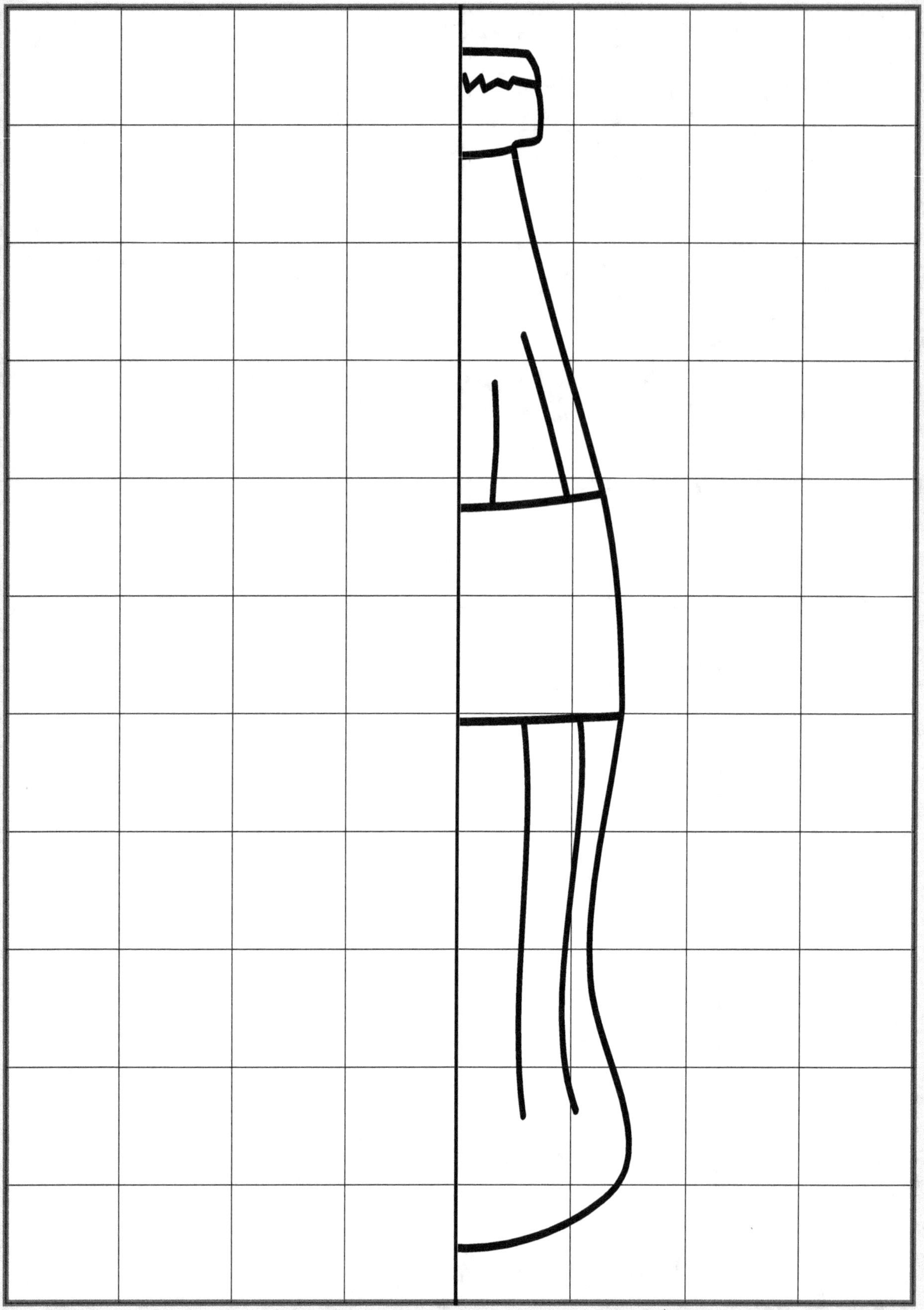

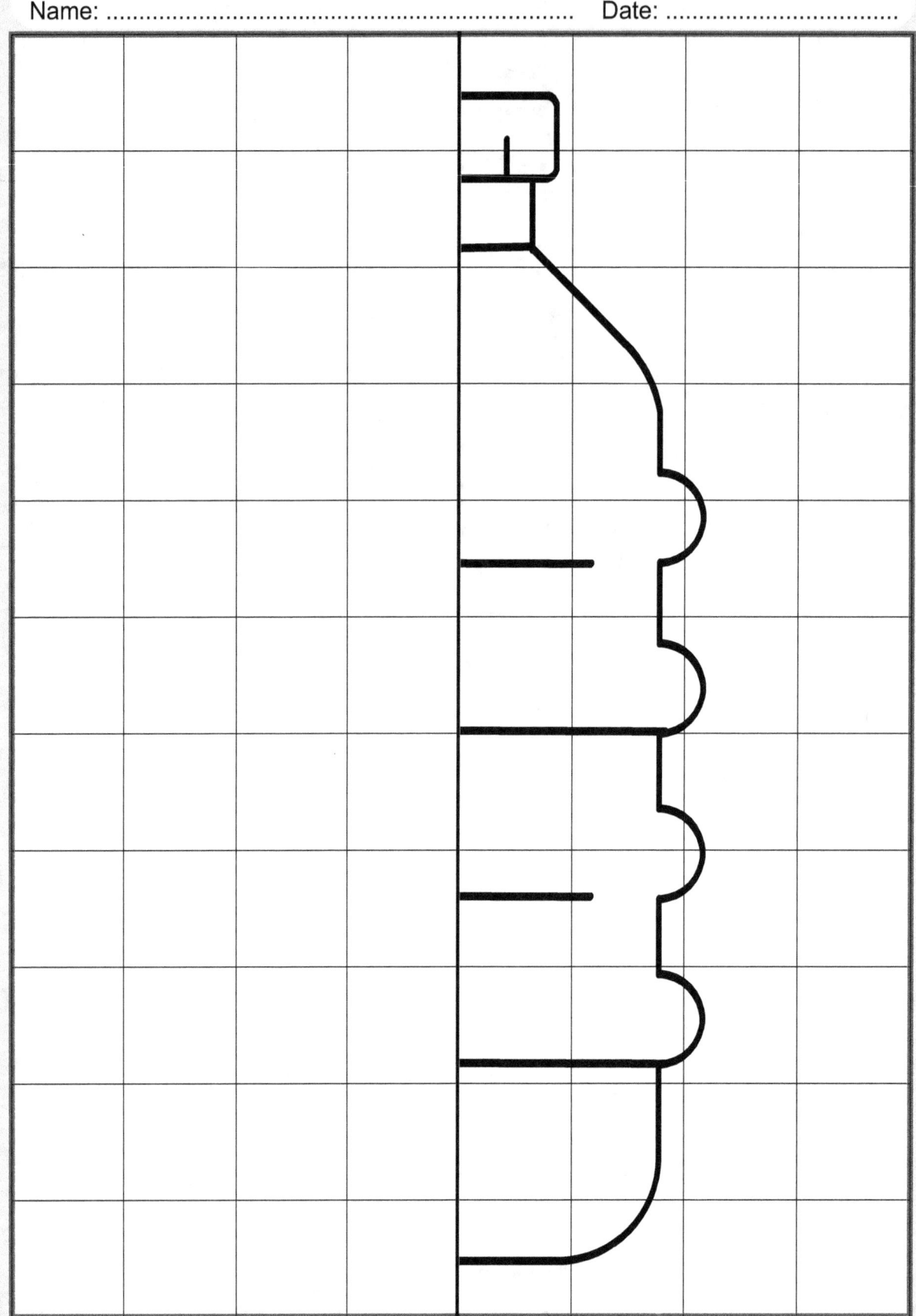

Name: .... Date: ....

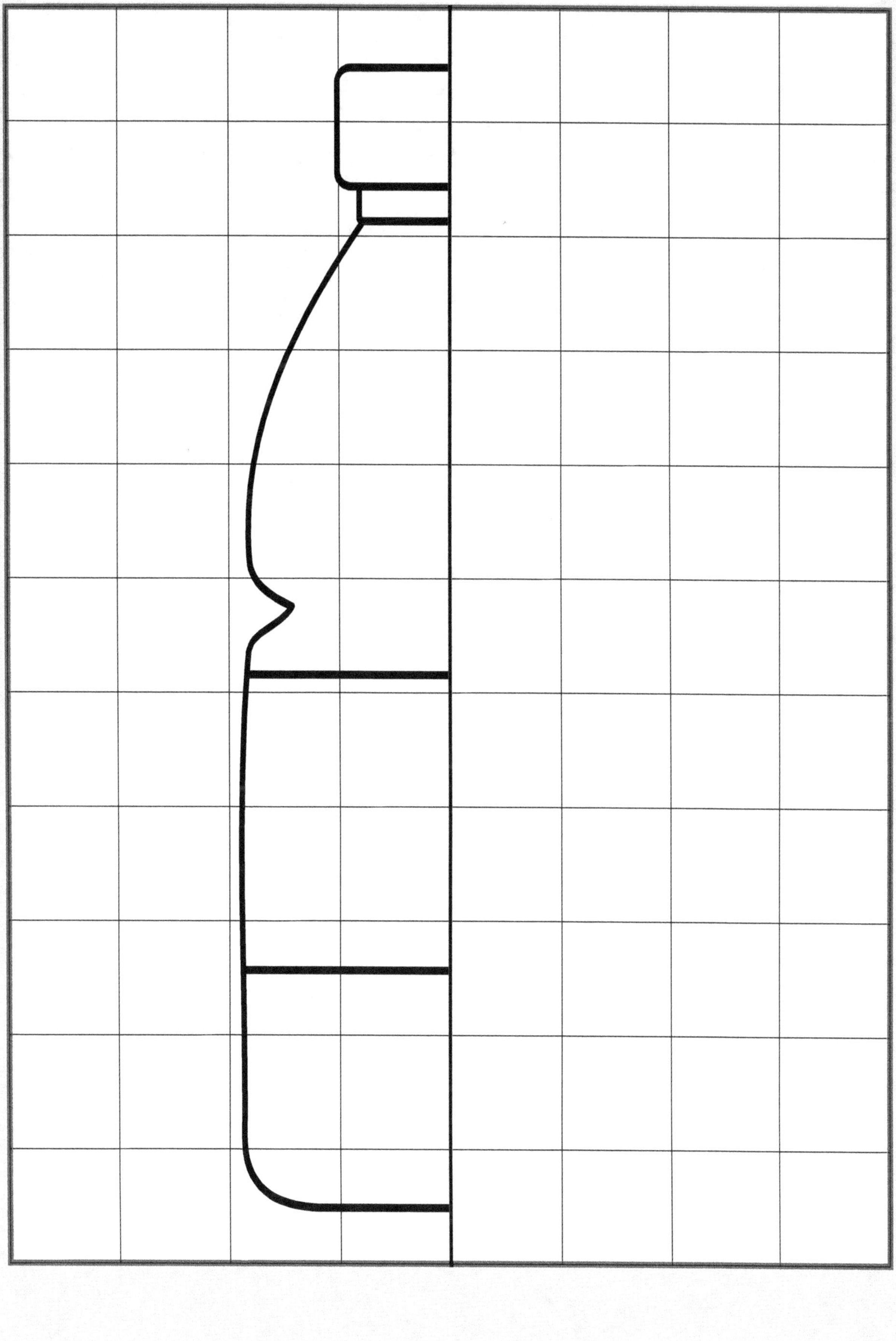

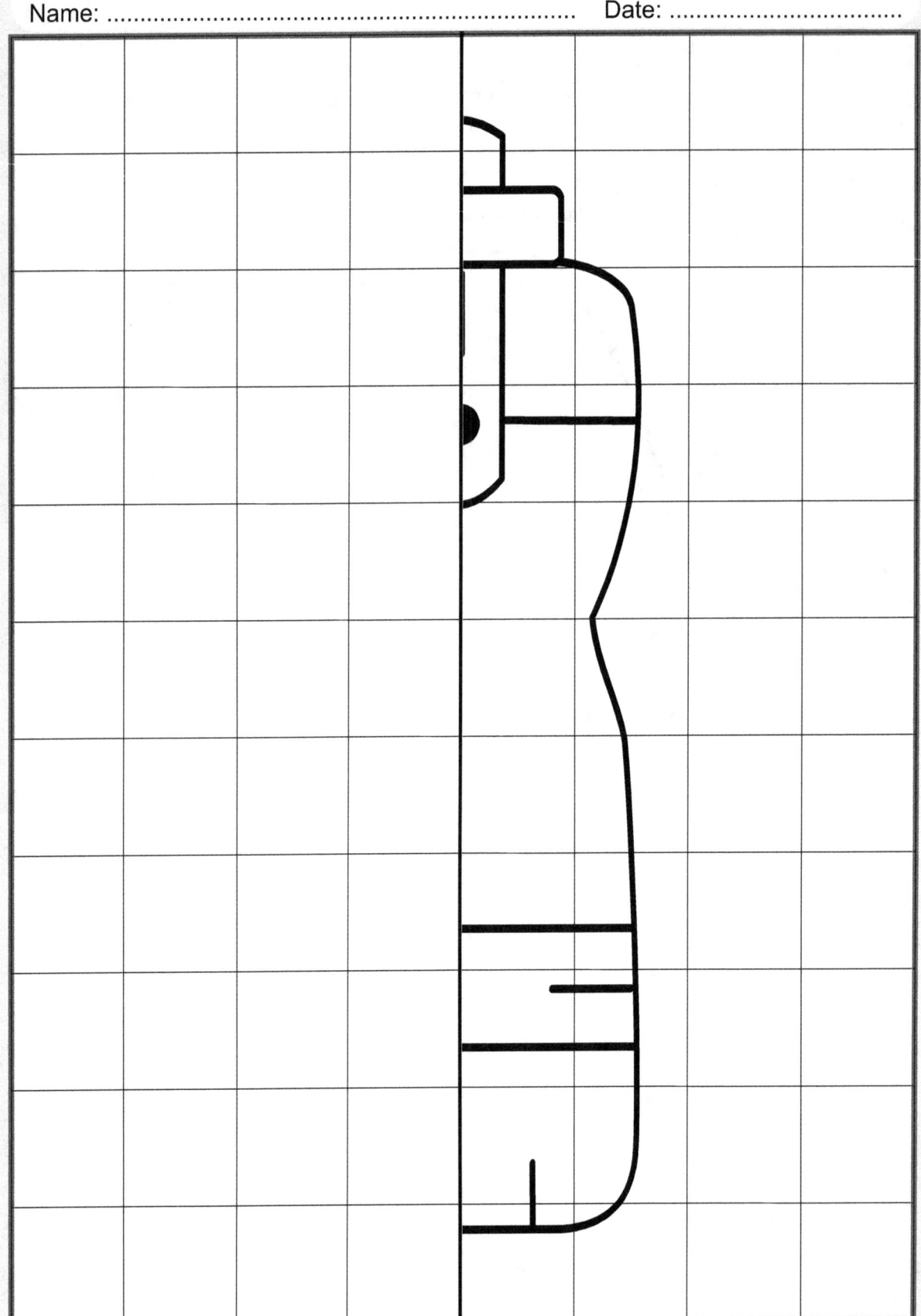

Name: .... Date: ....

Name: .... Date: ....

Name: .... Date: ....

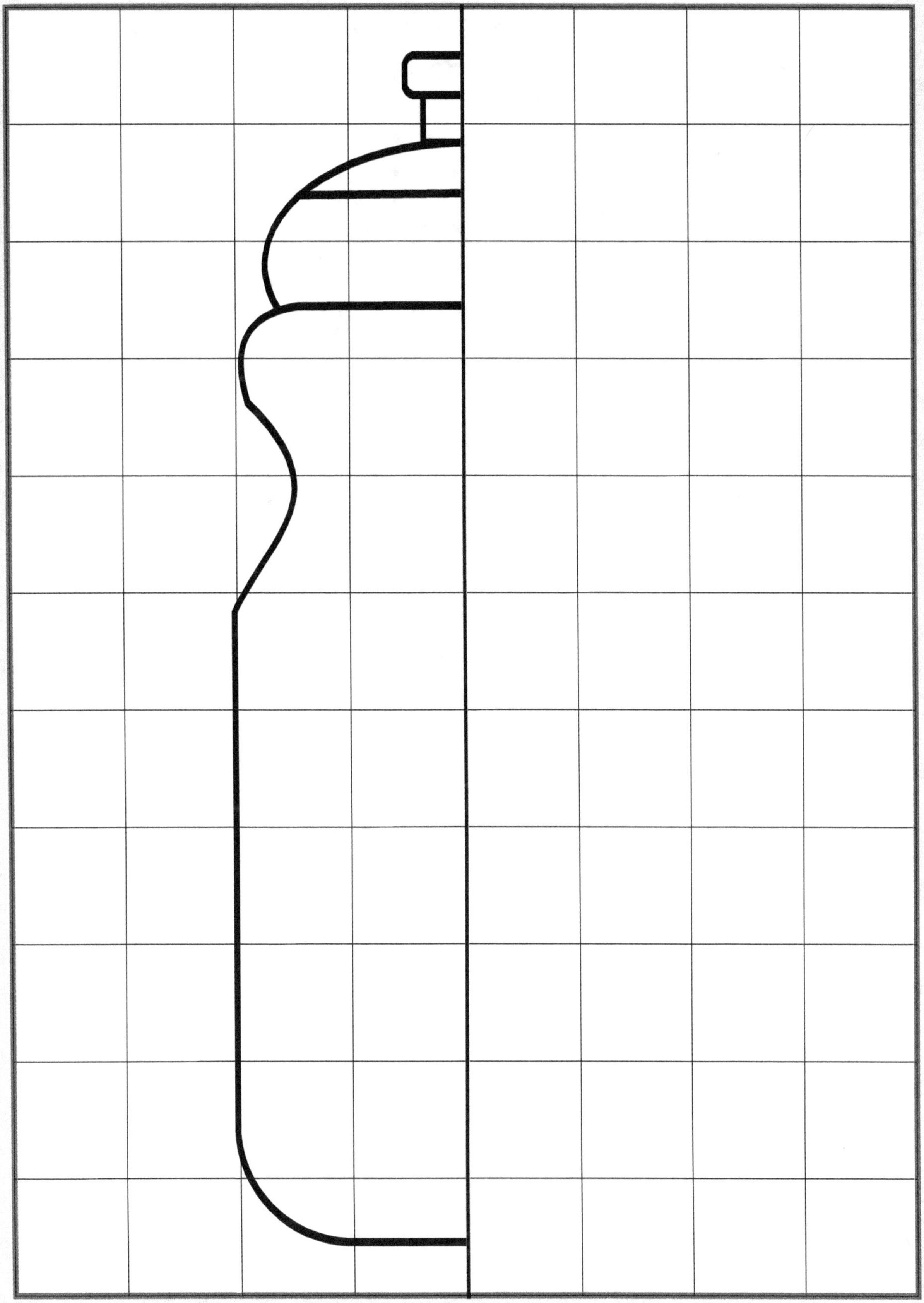

Name: .... Date: ....

Name: .... Date: ....

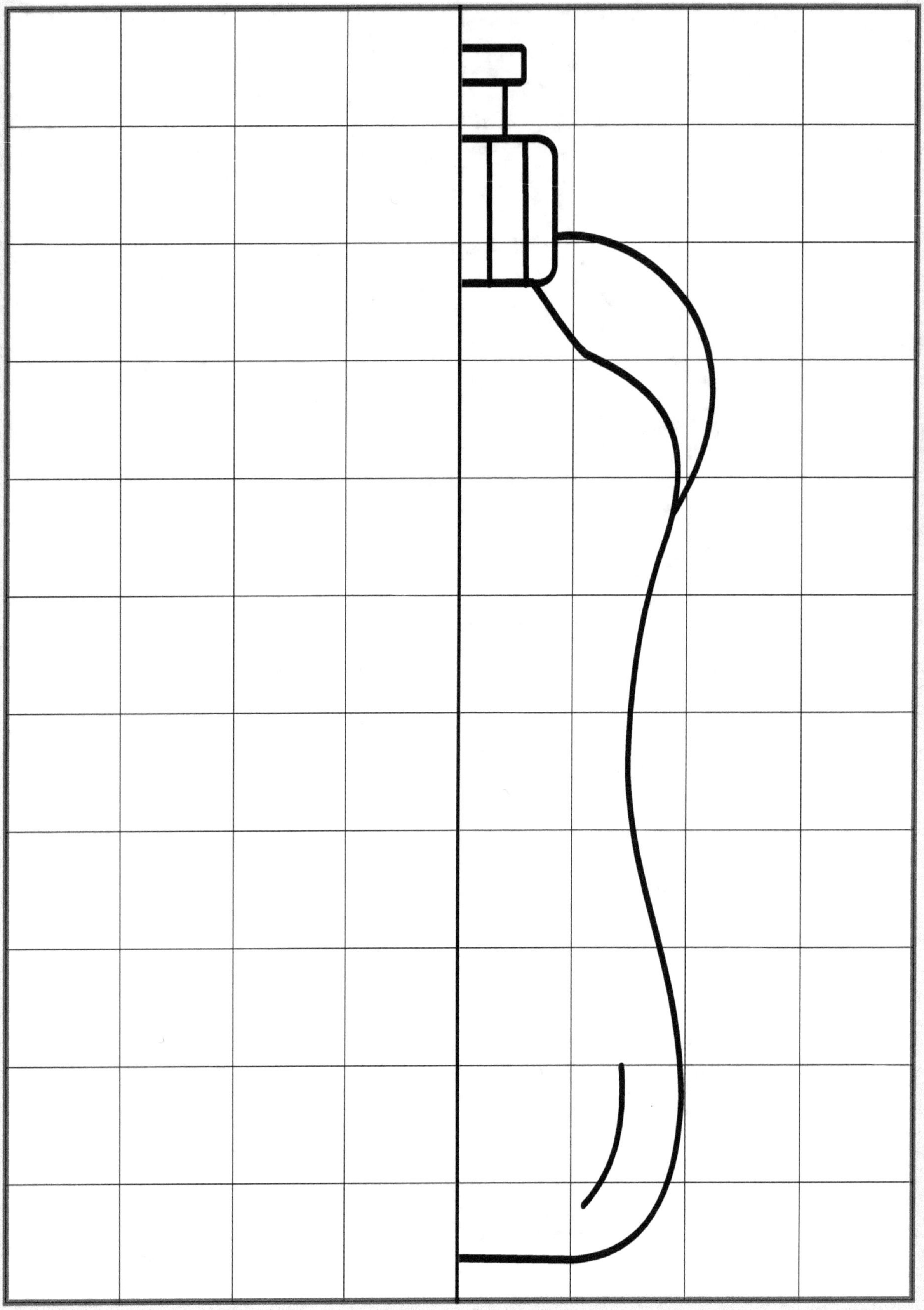

Name: .... Date: ....

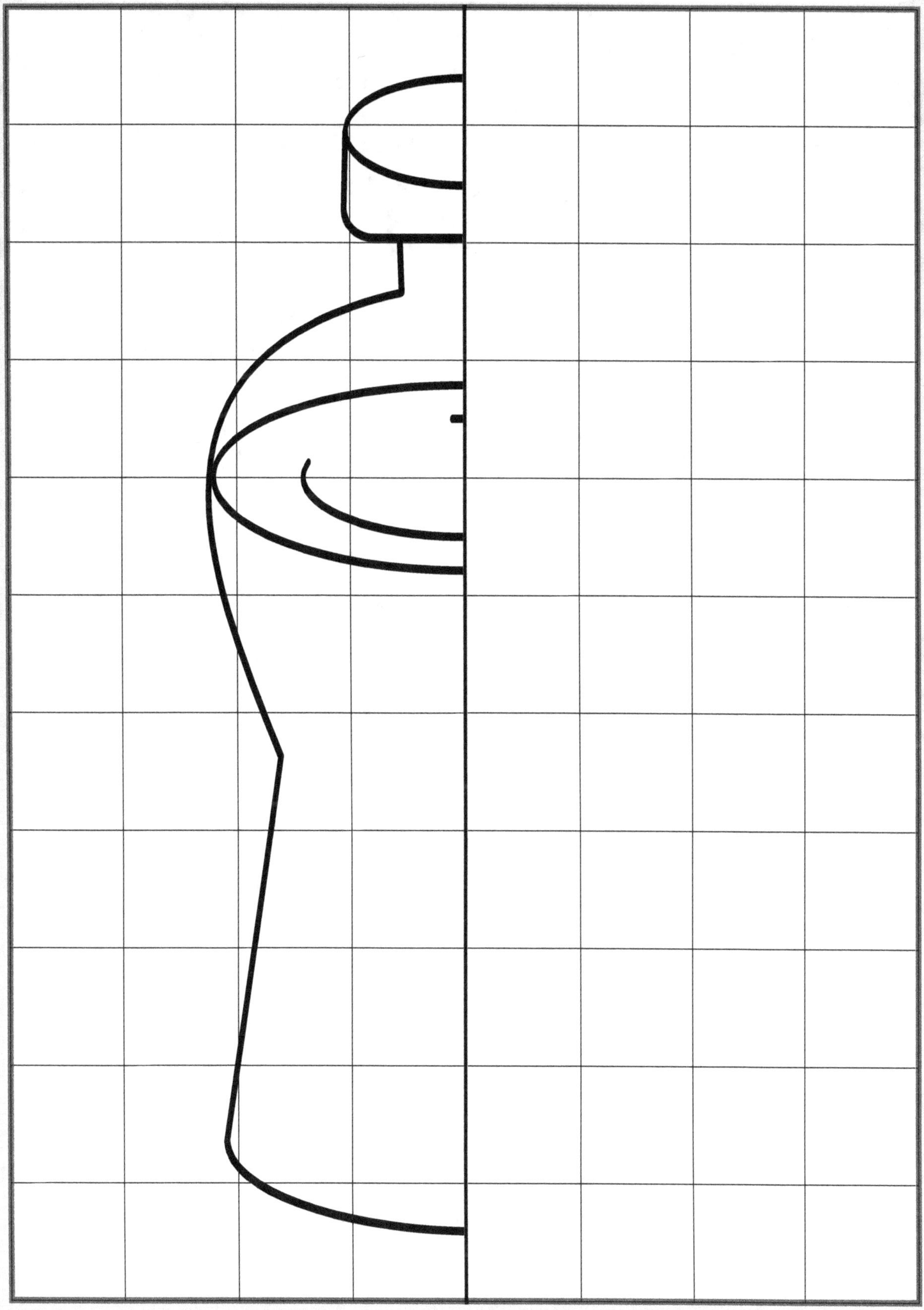

Name: .... Date: ....

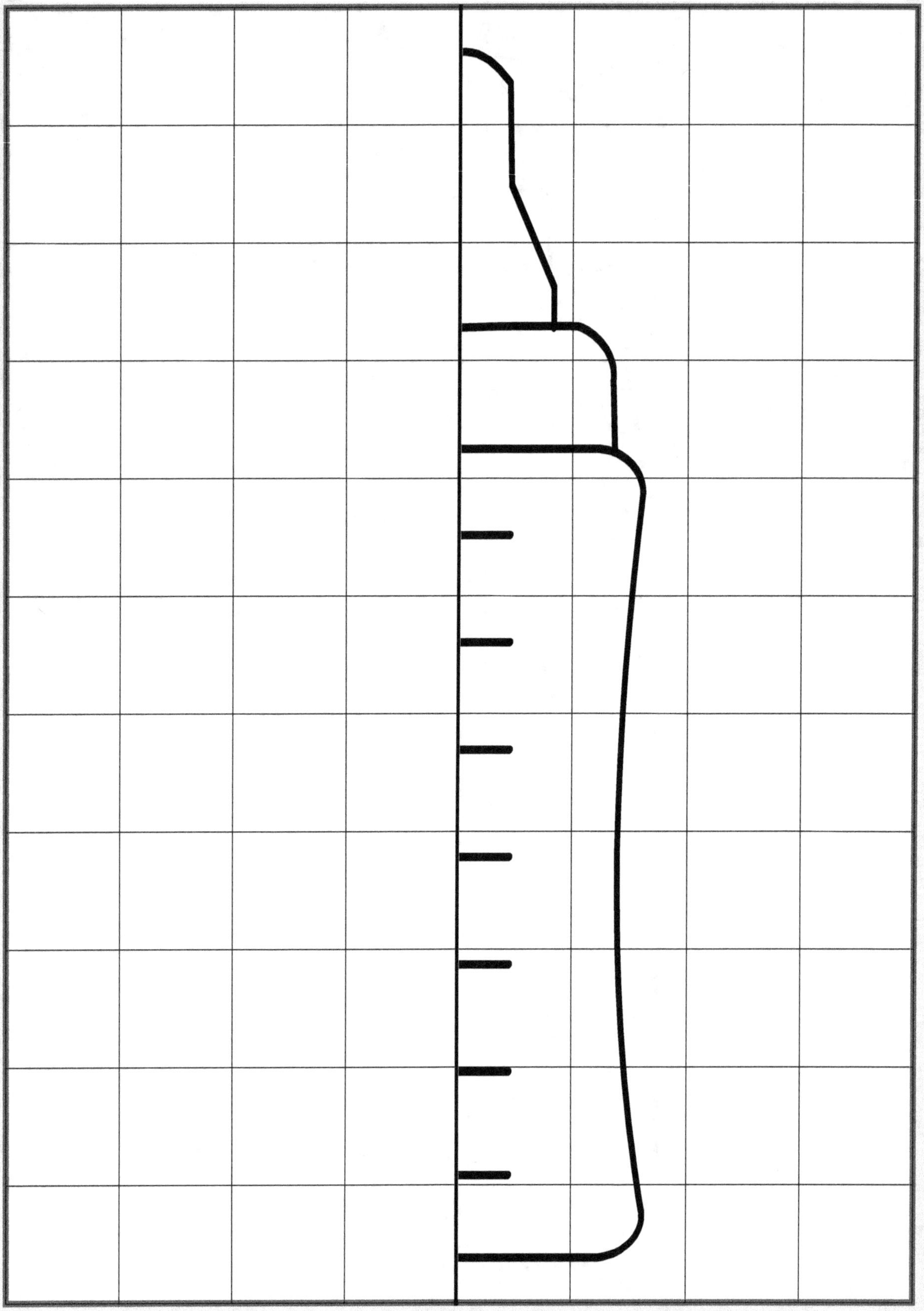

Name: .... Date: ....

Name: .... Date: ....

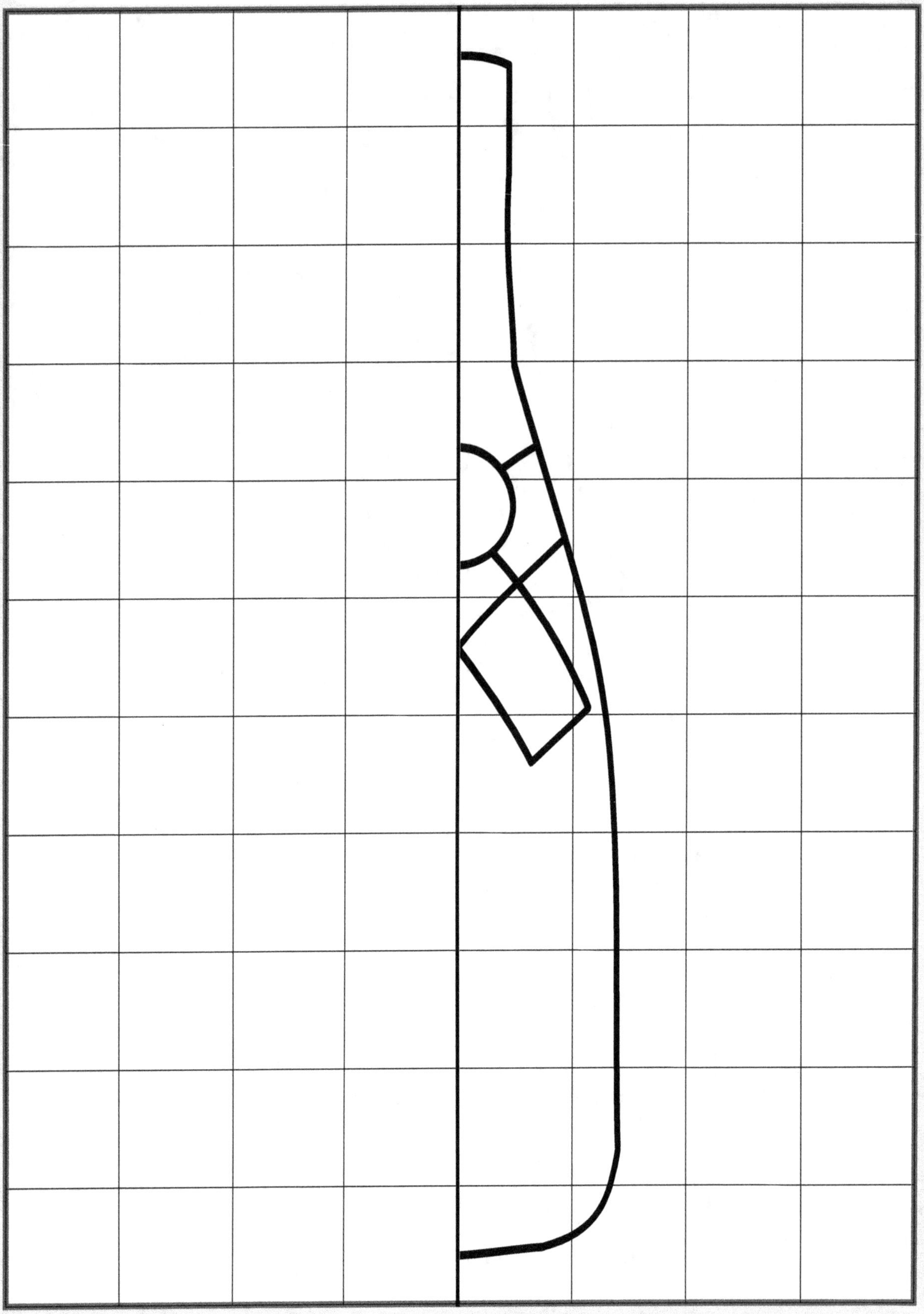

www.ingramcontent.com/pod-product-compliance
Lightning Source LLC
Chambersburg PA
CBHW081005220526
45467CB00008B/2706